Pizzas & Punk Potatoes

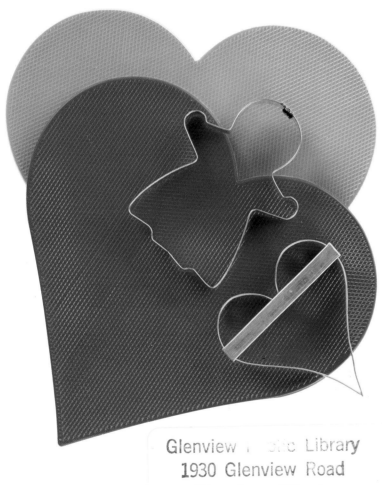

by Arielle Rosin
photographs by Daniel Czap
research by Etienne Collomb

series under the direction of Caroline Lancrenon

TICKNOR & FIELDS
New York · 1994

CONTENTS

PREFACE

Most of the chapters of *Pizzas & Punk Potatoes* first teach a recipe and then offer variations of it. Full instructions are given for the first recipe. Additionally, there are a few general rules of cooking that everyone should know:

• Read a recipe all the way through before starting to make it. Understand all the steps involved. Then put all the equipment and ingredients on the counter or table, ready to be used. It's annoying to be halfway through a project before finding out that important ingredients are missing. Of course, if there is something that must be kept very cold, it should be refrigerated until needed, but make sure all the ingredients are available.

• Measure carefully, especially when measuring ingredients for dough. A heaping cupful contains much more than a level cupful. Quantities in the recipes in this book are measured in level cupfuls and spoonfuls.

• Preheat the oven to the temperature called for. Ovens take time to heat, and food started in a cold oven might not cook properly.

Feel free to experiment with these recipes. Although some ingredients must be measured carefully or cooked according to the instructions—too much flour will make the pizza dough tough, and a potato boiled for too long will fall apart—everyone can make up new pizza shapes and toppings. And when making these recipes, don't worry if the results look different from the pictures! They'll still taste good.

EGG-MICE

Utensils
- small wooden skewer
- timer
- kitchen scissors
- paring knife
- cutting board
- apple corer
- small saucepan
- soup spoon

Ingredients (for 2 egg-mice)
- 1 large egg
- 2 slices of boiled ham
- 2 slices of cheese
- 2 lettuce leaves
- a bunch of chives

Put the egg in the saucepan and cover it with cold water. Bring the water to a boil and set the timer for 10 minutes. When the egg is cooked, remove it from the pan with the spoon. Place the egg under cold running water for a few seconds.

2

To remove the egg shell, tap the egg gently on a hard surface to crack the shell. When the egg is cool, peel off the pieces. Cut the egg in half lengthwise.

3

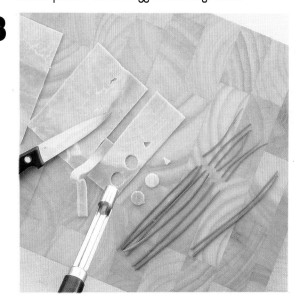

Cut two 1/2-inch-wide strips of ham and 2 small triangles. Use the apple corer to cut out 4 circles. Cut the tips off 12 sprigs of chives. Set aside 4 whole chives.

4

5

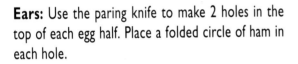

6

Ears: Use the paring knife to make 2 holes in the top of each egg half. Place a folded circle of ham in each hole.

Tail: Cut a 1/2-inch-long slit in the larger end of the egg halves and insert the strip of ham in each.

Nose: Cut out a small triangle at the smaller end of each egg half. Insert the triangular pieces of ham.

Eyes: Use the end of the wooden skewer to make 2 holes under the ears in each egg half. Gently insert a sprig of chive in each hole, then trim it, so that only a small piece of chive sticks out of hole.

Whiskers: Use the skewer to make 3 small holes on either side of each mouse's nose. Gently insert the cut (not pointed) end of a sprig of chive in each hole. Trim to about 1 inch long.

Serving: Use the apple corer to cut small circles of cheese. With the paring knife, cut two 1-inch squares of cheese, then cut the squares diagonally to make triangles.
Roll up the lettuce leaves and cut into small strips. Place each mouse on a serving dish. Arrange the cheese and lettuce around each mouse.

EGG-MUSHROOMS

Ingredients (for 1 mushroom)
- 1 large or jumbo egg
- 1 small tomato
- tube or small jar of mayonnaise
- a bunch of chives

Hard-boil the egg as instructed on page 9, and remove the shell. When egg cools, cut a slice off its larger end. Cut the tomato in half, remove the seeds from 1 half, and place it on top of the egg. Decorate the top of the tomato with drops of mayonnaise.

Make mini-mushrooms the same way but use half an egg, and top with half of a cherry tomato.

HEN AND CHICKS

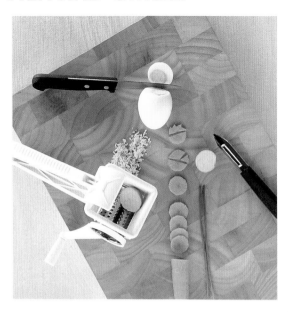

Ingredients (for 1 hen, 2 chicks)
- 1 large or jumbo egg and 2 medium eggs
- 1 carrot
- a bunch of chives
- yoke of another hard-boiled egg
- 1 lettuce leaf

Utensils
- rotary or straight hand grater

Hard-boil the eggs as instructed on page 9, and remove the shells. When eggs cool, cut a slice off larger end of each one. Peel the carrot and cut several thin slices from it.

Beak: Cut a slice of carrot in half, then cut each half into 3 triangles. Use 1 triangle for each of the beaks.

Crest: Cut 2 slices of carrot in half. Cut a zigzag along 1 edge to make the crest. Cut a long slit in the top of each egg and insert the crest and beak.

Eyes: Make the eyes as instructed for the egg-mouse, page 10.

To serve: Grate the egg yolk. Place the smaller eggs behind the large one on a serving plate. Arrange the egg yolk, chives, and lettuce on a plate.

> **E**ggs can be turned into other animal shapes. To make a rabbit, cut ears from the white of a hard-boiled egg, add a carrot triangle nose, chive whiskers, and egg yolk teeth. To make a porcupine, roll a slice of ham around the end of a hard-boiled egg, and insert thin sticks of carrot and cheese in the back.

THE EGG AS A SYMBOL

Eggs represent new life and the return of spring. They are used in the religious celebrations of many cultures and are mentioned in many sacred texts. Christians eat eggs at Easter to commemorate the resurrection of Christ and to celebrate the arrival of spring. Jews eat eggs at Passover, also in celebration of spring.

Eggs have been part of Easter celebrations for hundreds of years. In the past, Christians were forbidden to eat eggs during Lent, the forty days before Easter. All the eggs laid during that time had to be left to hatch or saved for Easter. At Easter, eggs were decorated and given to people, or hidden for children to find. A feast was prepared on Easter Sunday with special egg dishes. In one medieval cathedral, the bishop and the members of the choir threw eggs at each other during the Easter service!

The almost perfect shape of the egg has inspired painters, sculptors, and designers. To the left is an egg lamp designed in 1976 by Ben Wildness. Above is a still life with eggs by Jean-Baptist Chard (1699–1779).

THE EGG IN OTHER CULTURES

The creation myths of many cultures say that the world hatched from a special egg. In India, the Brahman religion (a form of Hinduism) says that the god Brahma created a Golden Egg with himself inside. When he broke out of the egg, he created the earth and the sky. The traditional Finnish creation story tells of a beautiful duck that laid seven eggs. The Mother of the Waters lifted her knee so that the duck would have a dry place to lay its eggs. When the eggs broke, a yolk became the sun, an egg white became the moon, and a piece of broken shell became the sky. In Papua New Guinea, the creation story says that people, animals, and vegetation hatched from the eggs of a turtle.

The Fabulous Fabergé Eggs

Easter is an especially important holiday in the Russian Orthodox Church. On this day, the priests and followers leave the church in a procession, led by children carrying icons. In the nineteenth century, a tradition began in Russia of exchanging decorated eggs on Easter. At first these were painted real eggs or eggs made of papier-mâché. Later in the century, wealthy people exchanged eggs of gold or silver. The rulers of Russia — the czars—gave the czarinas intricately jeweled and enameled eggs that opened to reveal a jewel or a beautifully detailed miniature model. The goldsmith Carl Fabergé, who created these eggs, became famous for them. Today, collectors prize Fabergé eggs as works of art.

The 100-Year-Old Egg

The Chinese consider 100-year-old eggs a delicacy. To make them, eggs are covered with tea leaves, lime, salt, and spices, and then are allowed to age—not for 100 years, but for about 100 days. The shell of a 100-year-old egg is the color of black marble. The egg looks hard-boiled, but its yoke is jade-green instead of yellow. The preserved eggs are quite unlike fresh eggs, just as pickles are unlike fresh cucumbers.

Eggs are high in cholesterol—approximately 210 milligrams per egg. But they also have great nutritional value. Eggs are rich in protein, sodium, and vitamins A, B_2, B_{12}, C, and E. The yolk is rich in iron.

Left: The Ostrich (1957), by Diego Giacometti, brother of Alberto Giacometti. This bronze sculpture supports a real ostrich egg. The statue is about 20 inches high. Ostriches lay the largest eggs, with an average diameter of 5 inches and weight of over 3 pounds. Decorated ostrich eggs were found in the royal tombs of Mesopotamia—they are 5,000 years old!

BUTTERFLY PIZZA

Utensils

- hand grater
- measuring cup
- rolling pin
- timer
- teaspoon
- tablespoon
- paring knife
- pastry wheel
- plastic spatula
- long metal spatula
- baking sheet
- pot holder
- cutting board
- large mixing bowl

Ingredients (dough for 4 individual pizzas, topping for 1)

- 1 package active yeast
- 3/4 cup warm water
- 2 cups all-purpose flour
- pinch of salt
- 6 tablespoons olive oil
- 1 small can (6 ounces) tomato sauce
- hot dog
- 1 small can (3 ounces) sliced mushrooms
- 2 or 3 small tomatoes
- mozzarella or another melting cheese,like Swiss or Gruyère

HOW TO KNEAD:

Place dough on a floured surface. Make the dough into a ball, and press down with the floured heels of the hands. Lift the ball and toss down on board, pushing it away with the hands. Massage the dough, turning it one-quarter around, and continuing to push, turn, and fold. The dough will become smooth and less sticky. It may be necessary to add more flour during the process.

1

Mix yeast and warm water in bowl. Wait 10 minutes. Add flour, salt, and oil. Mix. Knead for 10 minutes. Put in oiled bowl, cover, and put in warm place (75°–85° F) for 1 hour.

2

Place dough on a floured surface and punch out air bubbles. Divide it into 4 equal pieces.

3 Preheat oven to 400°F. Lightly flour the baking sheet and place 1 piece of dough in the center. Roll out the dough with rolling pin. Cut out the shape of a butterfly with the pastry wheel. Remove any excess dough with metal spatula and fingers.

TIP:
If mozzarella is very fresh, it will be too soft to grate. Instead, slice or tear into small pieces.

5

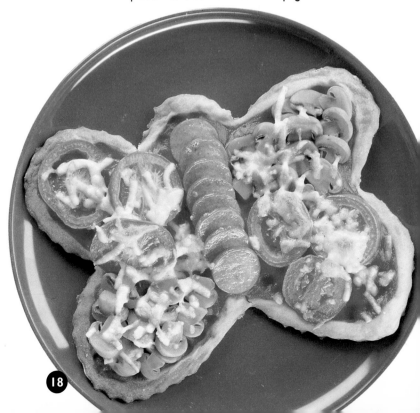

Slice the tomatoes and arrange on the other half of each wing. Grate the cheese and sprinkle it over pizza. Bake as instructed on page 19.

4

Spread the tomato sauce on the pizza, leaving a 1/2-inch border all around the edge. Cut the hot dog in thin slices and arrange down the center of the butterfly to form its body. Then place the mushrooms on half of each wing, as shown.

SUN PIZZA

Ingredients (for 1 individual pizza)
- pizza dough (page 17)
- 1 small can (6 ounces) tomato sauce
- 1 small can (7 ounces) corn
- 1/2 cup diced ham
- sliced red and green peppers
- a few cooked asparagus spears
- mozzarella
- 1 pitted black olive

TIP:
To dice means to cut up into small pieces or cubes.

Preheat the oven to 400° F. Roll out 1 piece of dough on a floured baking sheet and cut it into the shape of a sun with pastry wheel. Remove the excess dough. Spread the tomato sauce on the pizza almost to edges. Cover the sauce with corn, then with ham. Arrange the pepper strips and asparagus spears in a star pattern. Cut two 1-inch circles of cheese and place on the pizza. Slice olive in half and place in the center of each piece of cheese.

Preheat the oven to 400° F. Bake for about 20 minutes. Be careful taking the pan out of the oven: use a pot holder or ask an adult to help. Remove the pizza from the pan with a spatula. Let sit for 2–3 minutes before cutting and eating.

Mini-Pizzas

Utensils
- large cookie cutters

Ingredients (for 1 serving)
- pizza dough (page 17)
- 1 small can (6 ounces) tomato sauce
- 1 small tomato
- 3–4 pitted black olives
- 1 small can (7 ounces) corn
- mozzarella or other melting cheese
- 1/4 cup diced ham

Tip:
A pastry wheel or knife can also be used to cut out squares, triangles, circles, and many other shapes.

Preheat the oven to 400° F . Roll out 1 piece of the dough and cut with the cookie cutters. Remove excess dough.

Spread the tomato sauce on the dough almost to edges. Slice the tomato and olives. Arrange the tomatoes, corn, and olives on the pizzas. Grate or slice the mozzarella and sprinkle on top.

Bake for 10–15 minutes, or until dough is lightly brown. Remove pizza from oven (use pot holder) and let sit 2 minutes before serving.

It is easy to invent different kinds of pizzas. Top a fish-shaped pizza with tomato sauce, tuna, and shrimp. Top a heart-shaped pizza with tomato sauce, olives, and small heart-shaped pieces of cheese.

THE MARGHERITA PIZZA

Pizza Margherita was named for Marguerite of Savoy, who became the queen of Italy in 1878. A famous pizza chef, Raffaele Esposito, created three different kinds of pizza for the queen, but her favorite looked like the flag of Italy—red, green, and white. It was topped with fresh tomatoes, basil, and mozzarella.

THE ORIGINS OF PIZZA

No one knows exactly when pizza originated. Thousands of years ago, the Greeks and Romans sprinkled toppings such as oil, herbs, and cheese on flat bread, then heated it on a hearth. This early form of pizza had no tomato sauce, because there were no tomatoes in Europe then. After Spanish explorers brought tomatoes back from South America, pizza makers in Naples—then owned by Spain, not Italy—put tomatoes on their pizzas. They also continued to make pizza without tomato, which they still do.

The pizza usually eaten in the United States, topped with tomato sauce and cheese, was probably developed by Italian immigrants in the section of New York City called "Little Italy."

Below: The Bakers; terra cotta, Boeotia, Greece, seventh–sixth century B.C.

Above: The Pizzaïolo (pizza maker); Italy, about 1820.

Bread has been a nutritional staple for centuries. Depending on the type of flour used, bread can be a rich source of fiber to aid digestion. It also supplies iron, thiamine, niacin, and riboflavin.

BREAD

In ancient times, most meals consisted of flatbread (unleavened bread made of oats or barley meal, baked on a griddle or hot stone) and something to accompany the bread, such as garlic, onion, olives, vegetables, or a little meat or fish. Mexican tortillas, Middle Eastern pita, and Indian chapati are flatbreads. Early bread had to be flat.

Oats and barley are heated to separate the edible part of the grain from the inedible. Once the grain has been heated it will not interact with yeast and rise. Thus, leavened bread was not possible until people harvested wheat, the grain of which can be separated from its chaff without heating. The first leavened bread was probably made by accident, when wild yeast spores floated through the air and settled in a mixture of wheat and water.

THE TOMATO

The tomato is native to South America. It was originally a weed growing in corn and bean fields. By the 1500s, when the Spanish conquistadors arrived in South and Central America, the tomato was part of everyone's diet there. The Spanish brought the tomato back to Europe, and people planted it in their gardens, but not to eat. Most people thought tomatoes were poisonous so they were grown only for decoration. People in North America also thought the tomato was poisonous. One legend says that tomatoes were not accepted in the United States until Colonel Robert Gibbon Johnson ate a basket of them on the courthouse steps in Salem, New

Jersey, on September 26, 1820. He was determined to prove that tomatoes were safe. Thomas Jefferson grew them in his garden at Monticello, in Virginia, but only for private consumption.

The tomato is extremely rich in vitamins A, B, and C. Most varieties of tomato are very acidic, which makes them easy to home-process; the acid prevents the growth of harmful organisms.

WHO INVENTED THE SANDWICH?

People have put food on bread for thousands of years, but the word *sandwich* comes from Sir John Montagu, fourth earl of Sandwich (1718–1792). He liked to gamble. Refusing to leave the card table for meals, he asked his cook to bring him a piece of cold meat between two slices of bread. By the late 1800s, "sandwich" had entered the English language.

PUNK POTATO

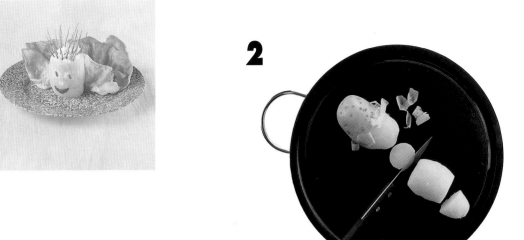

Utensils
- covered saucepan
- paring knife
- teaspoon
- fork
- skimming ladle or large slotted spoon
- timer
- cutting board
- bowl

Ingredients (for 1 potato)
- 1 large waxy potato
- a bunch of chives
- pinch of salt
- 1 tablespoon sour cream
- a little tomato sauce in a tube or ketchup in a squeeze bottle

2

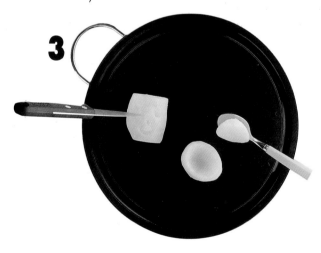

When the potato is cool enough to handle, peel it. Place peeled potato on a cutting board and slice off both ends. (It must be able to stand on one end.) Save the cut-off slices.

Place potato in saucepan filled with cold water. Add salt. Cover and bring to boil. Cook for 15–30 minutes after water begins to boil. Drain.

3

Carefully hollow out the inside of the potato with the teaspoon. Save the potato pulp. Use the paring knife to cut out 2 squares for eyes, a small square for a nose, and a crescent for a smile.

4

Cut up the chives as shown, but set aside the tips to make the hair.
Mash the potato pulp with the sour cream and diced chives.

5

Fill the inside of the potato with the mixture, and place a little in the eyes and nose. Arrange the chive tips on top to make hair. Put a small piece of chive in each eye. Fill the mouth with tomato sauce or ketchup.

For these recipes, use firm Eastern potatoes. Baking potatoes such as the Russet (Idaho) will become too crumbly. A fork inserted in the middle should go in easily, but do not overcook them.

POTATO PIG

TIP:
If the pretzels are too long, just break them in half.

Ears: Cut 2 slices from the hot dog. Cut a small triangle from each slice. Carefully cut a notch across the top of the potato and position the ears.

Snout: Cut another slice from the hot dog. Place some of the mashed potato mixture on the slice of hot dog and press it gently against the flattened end of potato.

Legs: Insert half-pretzels into the bottom so pig stands up.

Eyes: Follow the instructions for the egg-mouse eyes on page 10.

Ingredients (for 1)
- 1 large potato
- 1 slice of boiled ham
- 1 tablespoon sour cream
- 1 hot dog
- pretzel sticks
- chive sprig

Body: Cook the potato as instructed on page 25, and let cool. Peel and cut in half lengthwise. Cut off the tip at the smaller end.
Shred the ham with a grater.
Hollow out each potato half with a spoon. Mash the potato pulp with the sour cream and shredded ham. Refill each potato with the mixture and sandwich the 2 halves together.

LADYBUG POTATO

Ingredients (for 1)
- 1 large potato
- 1 medium tomato
- tomato sauce in a tube or ketchup in a squeeze bottle
- a bunch of chives
- 1 large lettuce leaf

Cut the potato in half, then cut a slice off the smaller end to make the head.

Arrange lettuce leaf on a plate, and place the potato on top. Put the head at the cut end of the potato as shown (page 29).

Cut the tomato in half and remove the seeds. Cut each half again. Place a tomato wedge on each side of the potato to make the wings.

Use a wooden skewer to make 2 holes in the top the head. Place a chive sprig in each hole to make the antennae.

Dot the top of the body with tomato sauce or ketchup.

CARROT-TOP

Ingredients (for 1)
- 1 large potato
- 1 small can of tuna, drained
- 1 tablespoon mayonnaise
- 1 medium carrot

To cook and shape the potato, see instructions for the punk potato on page 25.

Crumble the tuna with a fork.

Mash the potato pulp with the mayonnaise and tuna. Grate the carrot.

Stuff as instructed for the punk potato, using carrots for the hair instead of chives.

Use shredded chicken and mayonnaise to make a "curly-haired" potato with a few sprigs of parsley for the hair.

The Adventures of the Potato

In the early 1500s, the Spanish conquistadors landed in America and discovered a new vegetable, called *papas*, cultivated by the Indians of the Andes. At first, few Europeans would eat them because they thought potatoes would make them sick. The potato is a member of the nightshade family, which includes several poisonous plants; in fact, potato leaves are poisonous. Potatoes were only gradually accepted, but by the 1700s, they were an important crop throughout Europe. The potato was brought to Ireland in 1565 and became the staple food of the population, until a blight in 1845 infected the crop. This disease destroyed the entire potato crop for two years in a row. The great potato famine sent over one million Irish emigrants to America.

Ancient Freeze-Drying

By the 1500s, the Indians of Peru knew how to freeze-dry potatoes. The Peruvians harvested the potatoes and then spread them on the ground overnight to freeze. The next day, they walked on the potatoes, forcing the moisture out of them. This process was repeated for several days, resulting in dehydrated potatoes that could be stored for many years. This type of food preservation was not rediscovered until centuries later.

The potato is highly nutritious. One medium potato contains 3 grams of protein and 23 grams of carbohydrates. It is also high in fiber, vitamin C, vitamin B6, and niacin.

Above: Antoine Parmentier (1737–1813), a French apothecary (pharmacist), ate potatoes for the first time while he was a prisoner of war in Germany. After Parmentier convinced King Louis XVI and Queen Marie Antoinette to serve potatoes, the vegetable became part of the French diet. The king and queen also wore potato flowers as a decoration.

THE THOUSAND AND ONE WAYS TO COOK A POTATO

Potatoes can be boiled (with or without the skin), baked, fried in butter, deep-fried, prepared as a salad, mashed, scalloped, or stuffed. Modern methods of food preparation have expanded the potato's uses. Now it is made into potato chips, dehydrated potato flakes, dried soups, frozen French fries, or croquettes. There is only one way the potato is never eaten: raw.

MANY KINDS OF POTATOES

Different kinds of potatoes are best for different purposes. A dry, high-starch, "mealy" potato like the Russet is good baked or mashed, but it crumbles or becomes soggy when boiled. The Russet, America's most popular baking potato, is also called the "Idaho potato," but it is grown all over the country, not just in Idaho.

A moister, "waxy" potato is better for boiling or roasting. Many of these low-starch potatoes are smaller and rounder than Russets, and have smooth gold or red skin. They are sometimes called "Eastern potatoes."

Less well known, blue potatoes are an ancient variety that has recently captured people's attention. In South America, there are thousands of different potato varieties, with red, black, purple, green, and brown skins.

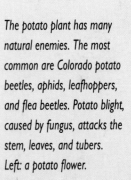

The potato plant has many natural enemies. The most common are Colorado potato beetles, aphids, leafhoppers, and flea beetles. Potato blight, caused by fungus, attacks the stem, leaves, and tubers. Left: a potato flower.

APPLE "SANDWICH"

Utensils
- 4 small wooden skewers (about 6 inches long)
- paring knife
- apple corer
- cutting board

Ingredients (for 1 sandwich)
- 1 slice of boiled ham
- 1 medium apple
- 4 pitted olives
- a piece of firm cheese (cheddar, Gruyère, gouda, or Swiss)

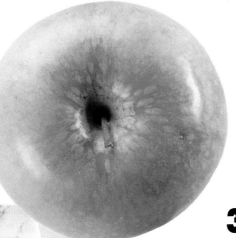

2

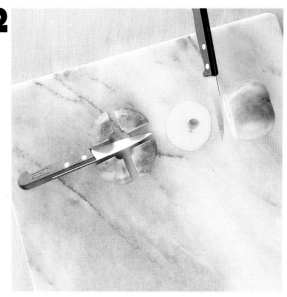

Cut a thick slice off the bottom of the apple. Cut the slice into quarters and set aside.

TIP:
Use 4 skewers to hold the apple together before dividing it into quarters.

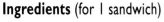

Place the apple on the cutting board and push the apple corer straight through the center. Twist corer and pull the core out.

3

Cut the rest of the apple into 3 equal slices. Set apple upright on cutting board and cut downward, dividing apple into 4 equal sections. 1 skewer holds each together.

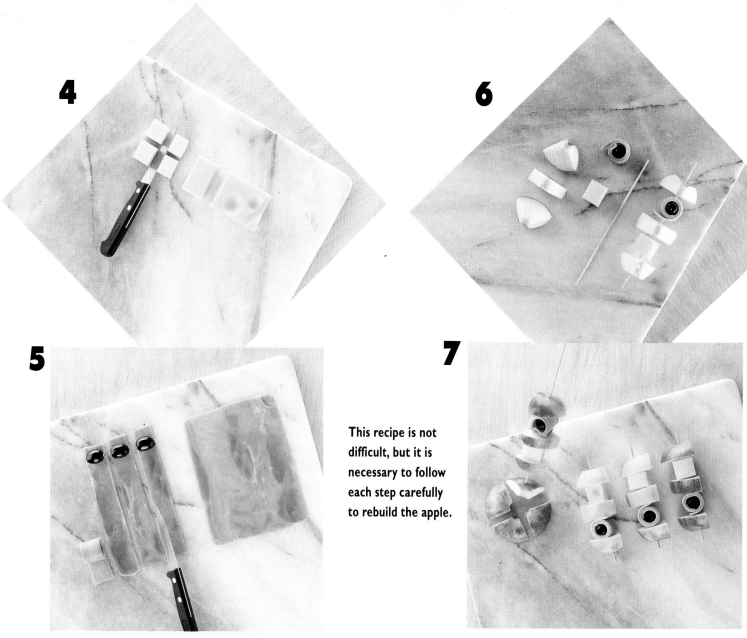

4

5

6

7

This recipe is not difficult, but it is necessary to follow each step carefully to rebuild the apple.

Cut 4 cubes of cheese, each about 3/4 inch.
Cut 4 strips of ham about 3/4-inch wide. Place an olive at the end of each strip, and roll up the strip, starting at the end with the olive.

Remove the pieces of apple from 1 skewer. Slide a piece of apple (its top) on the skewer, then a strip of ham, a second piece of apple, a cube of cheese, and a third piece of apple. Repeat for each skewer. Insert each skewer into one of the quarters cut from the bottom of the apple. The skewers should now stand upright. Arrange them in a circle on a plate to serve (see photo).

CARAMEL APPLE

Utensils
- frying pan
- skimming ladle or
  large slotted spoon
- saucepan
- timer
- paring knife
- tablespoon
- cutting board

Ingredients (for 1)
- 1/4 cup sliced almonds
- 1 apple
- 2 tablespoons sugar
- caramel candies or
  caramel sauce

TIP:

If apple is firm,
it may be easier to
insert almond
slivers (matchstick
slices).

Toast the almonds in a frying pan over low heat.
Let cool.

Peel the apple and set the stem aside. Place the
apple in the saucepan and cover it with cold water.
Add sugar and bring to a boil. Cook for 10 minutes. Remove the apple with the skimming ladle
and let it drain. Place the apple on a plate and let
cool for 10 minutes.

Carefully insert almond slices into apple all around
the bottom and return it to the plate.

Melt caramels over low heat or make caramel
sauce (see box). Pour caramel sauce over the top
of the apple and reinsert the stem.

To make caramel sauce, place 4 tablespoons of
sugar and 1 tablespoon of water in a small saucepan.
Cook over very low heat, stirring occasionally, until sugar
liquefies and turns light brown, about 10 minutes.
Caution: melted sugar is very hot; be careful pouring.

CHOCOLATE APPLE

Utensils
- 2 saucepans of different sizes or double boiler
- cooling rack
- paring knife
- apple corer
- long metal spatula
- fork
- cutting board

Ingredients (for 1)
- 7 ounces (7 squares) semisweet chocolate
- 1 large apple
- cake decorations:
  icing flowers
  silver candy balls
  multicolored sprinkles
- 2 marzipan leaves

DOUBLE BOILER:
This consists of a smaller saucepan resting inside a larger saucepan. Hot water in the lower pan slowly heats the food in the upper one. Food heated in a double boiler will not burn.

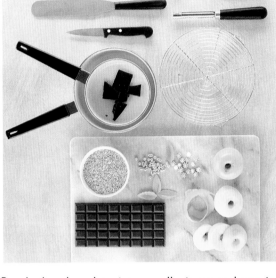

Break the chocolate into small pieces and put in small saucepan. Place this saucepan in a larger one containing hot water and simmer water until chocolate is melted. Core and peel the apple, and cut it horizontally into 3 slices. Remove melted chocolate from stove and use a fork to dip a piece of apple in the chocolate. Make sure it is completely coated on all sides. Remove, place on the rack, and quickly sprinkle the decorations all around the edges.

Repeat for the other 2 apple slices.

Let the apple pieces dry on the rack for approximately 30 minutes.

Rebuild the apple on a plate. Insert marzipan leaves on the top. (Or make paper leaves and don't eat them.)

An apple makes a delicious dessert cup. Cut apple in half, hollow it out, and fill with fruit salad, whipped cream, or ice cream. A little lemon rubbed on the apple's cut surfaces keeps it from turning brown.

THE FORBBIDEN FRUIT

The apple has been known for thousands of years and appears in the mythology, legends, and fairy tales of many civilizations. Snow White's stepmother tried to poison her with an apple, the hero Paris gave the Greek goddess Aphrodite a golden apple and started the Trojan War—and Adam and Eve ate an apple from the Tree of Knowledge and were expelled from the Garden of Eden. The Bible, however, mentions only a fruit, not specifically an apple. So, how did the apple become the fruit of knowledge?

THE NAME OF THE APPLE

In Latin, the word *pomum* means a fruit with seeds or a pit. In the Middle Ages, the meaning of *pomum* in French grew to mean only the apple. In other languages, such as Romanian, it still means simply "fruit." So early Latin translators of the Bible used the word *pomum* to mean fruit, and it was later misunderstood to refer to the apple.

AN APPLE A DAY

People say "an apple a day keeps the doctor away." This an old tradition. Since ancient times, people have believe that apples are a source of long life and health. Whe Alexander the Great (356–323 B.C.) was looking for th Fountain of Youth, he met priests who ate nothing b apples. They claimed that the fruit allowed them to live se eral hundred years! In the Middle Ages, people often ate apple after a meal—not to keep the doctor away, but clean their teeth. Toothbrushes hadn't been invented yet.

APPLE ORCHARDS REQUIRE SPECIAL CARE

Commercial apples are harvested from grafted trees. The varieties are rarely grown from seed because the trees produced from the seed may grow too slowly or catch diseases too easily. To produce McIntosh apples, for instance, a farmer may attach McIntosh branches onto another kind of fruit tree—one that does not grow as big or that is resistant to disease. This grafting allows farmers to produce the kind of apples they want more easily and with fewer problems.

Opposite, top: The Son of Man, *by Belgian painter René Magritte (1898–1967).*
Opposite, bottom: Adam and Eve, *by English painter William Strang (1859–1921.)*

Seven thousand varieties of apples have been recorded throughout the world. No one person is likely ever to see them all, but chances are everyone is familiar with some of the most common varieties.

The Golden Delicious, a sweet apple that ripens to a lovely yellow color, is the most widely grown variety, representing 65 percent of the global consumption. It was developed in West Virginia, at the end of the nineteenth century. Red Delicious apples are also widely grown.

The McIntosh is a red, medium-tart dessert apple. The Jonathan is spherical in shape, deep red, and tart.

Winesap apples are tart and deep red. They are used for cooking and eating.

The Granny Smith is a large, tart, green apple that was developed in Australia, but is now grown in the United States.

The Star Apple, named for its unusual shape, dates from the Middle Ages.

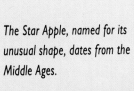

COOKING APPLES, EATING APPLES

Besides being eaten raw, apples are made into pies, applesauce, jelly, cider, and many other products. They are baked, stewed, fried, dried, frozen, and pressed. Certain varieties of apple are better for particular purposes. Eating (also called "dessert") apples, such as the McIntosh, are enjoyed raw, but can become too soft—or even burst—when baked. A Rome Beauty, on the other hand, bakes well, but is not as good to eat.

GIFT-WRAPPED CREPES

Utensils

- 2 saucepans of different sizes or double boiler
- soup spoon
- whisk
- rolling pin
- measuring cups
- small ladle
- paring knife
- metal spatula
- timer
- pastry wheel
- 10-inch nonstick frying pan
- cutting board
- 2 large bowls
- aluminum foil

Ingredients (for about 12)

- 2 cups all-purpose flour
- 2 cups milk
- 3 large eggs
- 2 tablespoons oil
- 1/4 teaspoon vanilla extract
- 2 tablespoons sugar
- pinch of salt
- 8 ounces (8 squares) semisweet chocolate
- 1 package (8 ounces) almond paste
- green and red food coloring
- silver candy balls

TIPS:

Add the vanilla and sugar only when making crepes with sweet fillings. Crepes are much thinner than American pancakes, so the batter is thin, too. Add a little milk just before cooking if the batter is too thick. It should be the consistency of heavy cream.

1

Put the flour in mixing bowl and make a well in the center. Pour in 1 cup of milk. Mix until there are no lumps. Beat the eggs in separate bowl, and add them to the flour and milk. Mix well. Then add the oil, vanilla, sugar, and salt. Gradually add the remaining milk while mixing. Let the batter stand for at least 1 hour.

2

To oil the pan, pour 1–2 teaspoons of oil into the cold pan. Use a paper towel to rub the oil all around. If the pan becomes too dry after making several crepes, add a little more oil, but do not spread it with the towel because the pan will be hot.

Preheat the oven to 200° F. Oil the pan. Heat pan and pour 1 ladle of batter in its center. Tilt it so that the batter covers the entire bottom. When the edges start to curl up, turn the crepe with spatula. Cook for 1–2 minutes on the other side. Put crepe on a plate and make more, stacking them on plate. Cover plate with foil and place in warm oven.

3

Break the chocolate into pieces and melt it in a double boiler above hot water. Put a spoonful of the melted chocolate on each crepe and spread it gently, to within I inch of the edge.

4

Fold 2 sides of the crepe to the center. Fold in half again to form a package, as shown.

MELTING CHOCOLATE:

Put the chocolate in a small saucepan or bowl. Place this into a larger saucepan containing hot water. Cook over a low heat; the hot water melts the chocolate slowly without burning.

5

To serve: Divide the almond paste in half. Rub a few drops of food coloring into each half. Roll out with the rolling pin. Cut into strips with the pastry wheel.

Lay I strip of each color almond paste on a plate, I across the other. Place the crepe on them and wrap their ends over the package. Push silver candy balls into the almond paste for decoration.

Note: Strings of licorice candy can also be used to tie packages.

CREPE CONES

Ingredients (for 12)
- 1 pint strawberries
- 2 kiwis
- 1 cup raspberries
- crepe batter
  (page 41)
- whipped cream

Wash the strawberries and raspberries. Remove the hulls from the strawberries. Peel the kiwis. Cut the kiwis and strawberries into 1/2-inch slices.
Cook the crepes as instructed on pages 41–42, and let them cool. Set aside a few crepes. Fold each of the remaining crepes in half and then into thirds to make cones. Fill each cone with fruit.
Slice a strip from another crepe and wrap it around the base of each cone. Spoon whipped cream onto the top of the fruit.

FRUIT FAVORS

Ingredients (for 12)
- crepe batter (page 41)
- green food coloring
- red food coloring
- jam (any flavor)
- several strings of licorice candy

Place half the crepe batter in 1 bowl and half in another. Color one batch with a few drops of red food coloring and the other with green. Mix each well. Cook the crepes as instructed on pages 41–42. Spread a spoonful of jam on each crepe. Roll up and tie the ends with a string of licorice candy, as shown.

SAVORY CREPE ROLLS

Ingredients
- crepe batter without sugar and vanilla (page 41)
- 7 ounces taramasalata (or whipped cream cheese)
- 3 ounces salmon roe (or minced red bell pepper)
- 3 ounces black lumpfish roe (or minced green bell pepper)

Make 6 crepes. Spread each with a layer of taramasalata, a Greek cod roe mixture. Sprinkle a line of roe along one side of each crepe and roll up, starting with the edge with the roe. Cut each roll into 1-inch sections.

TO BLANCHE
Plunge food briefly into boiling water— for about half a minute—and then rinse with cold water.

CREPE PURSES

Ingredients (for 12)
- crepe batter made without sugar and vanilla (page 41)
- 1 medium avocado
- 4 tablespoons cream cheese at room temperature
- 4 tablespoons mayonnaise
- 1 lemon, cut in half
- 1 can (4 1/4 ounces) tiny shrimp
- a bunch of chives, blanched

Make the crepes as instructed on pages 41–42. Peel the avocado, cut in half, and remove the pit. Cut each half into 4 pieces and then into cubes, as shown. Sprinkle lemon juice on avocado so it does not turn brown.

Mix the cream cheese and mayonnaise. Add the shrimp and avocado, and blend well.

Place a spoonful of this mixture in the center of each crepe. Gather up the edges of the crepe to form a pouch and tie the edges closed with 2 blanched chives, or use kitchen string.

A PANCAKE FOR EVERY TASTE

A version of the pancake, or crepe, exists in almost every culture. All over the world, pancakes are eaten alone or as an accompaniment to other food. The French eat crepes like the ones made in the previous recipes, but the Brittany crepe, made of buckwheat, is also a specialty. In the Far East, some pancakes contain scallions. In Russia, blini—thick pancakes of buckwheat flour—are eaten with sour cream and caviar or salmon. Norwegian or Swedish pancakes are spread with lingonberries. Austrian and German sweet pancakes puff up. And, the thick buttermilk pancakes of the United States are served for breakfast with butter and jam or syrup.

Village near Lake Chad, Nigeria. In Africa, flat cakes are made from ground millet, a small round seed.

GRAINS AND CEREALS

Pancakes are made of flour, which is ground from any of several types of grain. Grains are the edible part of plants such as wheat, oats, buckwheat, and corn. These plants, as a group, are called "cereals." The word *cereal* comes from Ceres, the Roman goddess of agriculture, who taught human beings how to grow plants. Almost all ancient cultures had myths to explain the beginning of cultivation, because the ability to grow food—and not depend on wild plants—was so important to early civilizations.

Illuminated manuscript page from The Book of Hours of the Duchess of Burgundy, *illustrating the making of crepes (left).*

Right: A French baker's sign showing a wheat sheaf, eighteenth century.

Left: A painting by Mexican painter Diego Rivera (1886–1957), illustrating the different stages of corn cultivation, from the planting of the seed to the making of tortillas. Tortillas are a flatbread similar in appearance to pancakes.

THE STORY OF CREPES SUZETTE

repes Suzette are crepes served with a sauce of orange juice, lemons, but-
r, vanilla, sugar, and brandy. As the dessert is served, the sauce is set on
e. According to one story, this dessert was created at the Café de Paris in
Monaco, in the late 1800s. Edward, prince of Wales, was having lunch with
young French woman. As the chef prepared the dessert, its sauce caught
re. The chef was afraid the dessert was ruined, but he tasted it and
ecided it was great. The prince liked the crepes so much that the chef
anted to honor the prince by naming the dish after him. The future king
raciously refused and suggested they be named for his dining companion.
nd they were—at least according to this version of the story.

47

Buckwheat and whole wheat flours are rich in potassium, a mineral essential for the proper functioning of the kidneys, heart, and muscles. All-purpose white flour has had the kernel and bran removed before grinding, but it is enriched with calcium and vitamins to replace some of the nutrients lost in refining.

STRAWBERRY MILKSHAKE

Utensils

- measuring cup
- electric drink mixer
  or blender
- paring knife
- ice cream scoop
- fork
- teaspoon
- small wooden skewers
- pastry brush
- colored straws
- tablespoon
- soda glass
- cutting board
- small bowl

Ingredients (for 1 drink)

- 1 medium egg
- colored sprinkles
- 1 cup very cold milk
- 1 tablespoon plain yogurt
- 1 scoop strawberry ice cream
- 2 strawberries

1

To decorate the glass:

Separate the egg yolk from the white; discard yolk. Beat the egg white in small bowl with a fork. Dip the pastry brush in the egg white and draw a design on the outside of the glass.

2

Shake sprinkles over side of the glass. Tap the glass gently to remove excess.

> **A** blender can be used if a drink mixer is not available. Put lid firmly on top before turning the machine on.

3

5

Wash the strawberries and remove their hulls. Cut a notch in each berry and insert wooden skewer. Place in drink. Insert a colored straw.

4

Pour the milk into the measuring cup or blender container. Add the yogurt and ice cream, and whirl for several seconds. Pour the milkshake into the decorated glass.

VANILLA MILKSHAKE

Ingredients (for 1)
- 1 cup very cold milk
- 1 tablespoon plain yogurt
- 1 scoop vanilla ice cream
- chocolate sprinkles
- crushed hazelnuts
- small meringues or soft candies

Use milk, yogurt, and ice cream to prepare the milkshake as instructed on page 50. Pour into a glass, then add chocolate sprinkles and hazelnuts on top.
Slide the meringues onto a wooden skewer and place in the glass.
Add a colored straw.

CHOCOLATE MILKSHAKE

Ingredients (for 1)
- 1 medium egg, separated and yolk discarded
- dried coconut flakes
- 1 cup very cold milk
  - 1 tablespoon plain yogurt
  - 1 scoop chocolate ice cream
- coconut candies
- icing leaves

Dip the pastry brush in beaten egg white and brush a line around the top of the glass. Turn it over and dip it in a bowl of grated coconut.
Prepare the milkshake with milk, yogurt, and ice cream as instructed on page 50, and pour it into the glass.
Alternate coconut candies and sugar leaves on wooden skewer.
Place the skewer and straw in the glass.

PISTACHIO MILKSHAKE

Ingredients (for 1)
- 1 cup very cold milk
- 1 tablespoon plain yogurt
- 1 scoop pistachio ice cream
- soft candies
- marshmallows

Using the milk, yogurt, and ice cream, prepare the milkshake as instructed on page 50.
Slide the candies and marshmallows onto the wooden skewer. Place the skewer and straw in the milkshake.

It is easy to create all sorts of milkshakes using various kinds of fruit and candy decorations and different flavors of ice cream. Try banana, raspberry, strawberry, or coffee ice cream. Use frozen yogurts, too.

TROPICAL MILKSHAKE

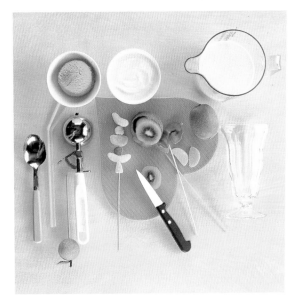

Ingredients (for 1)
- 1 cup very cold milk
- 1 tablespoon plain yogurt
- 1 scoop mango, passion fruit, or other tropical ice cream
- assorted jelly candies
- 1 kiwi

Using the milk, yogurt, and ice cream, prepare the milkshake as instructed on page 50.
Slide the candies on the wooden skewer.
Place the skewer and straw in the milkshake.
Peel and slice the kiwi. Cut a notch in 1 slice and attach to the rim of the glass.

Vanilla: The Plant and The Flavoring

Vanilla flavoring comes from an orchid that grows in the tropics. The plant has fleshy leaves, white flowers, and green seedpods. While it is growing, it has almost no smell. The seedpods (also called vanilla beans) are picked just as they become ripe, dipped in boiling water, and then slowly dried in the sun, protected by blankets or boxes. As the beans age, they turn dry and brown, and crystals form on the outside of the pods. These crystals contain vanillin, which is responsible for vanilla's characteristic smell and taste.

Vanilla reached Europe from the Central America about the time of the Spanish conquest in the sixteenth century. The Aztecs used vanilla as a flavoring for chocolate drinks. Vanilla is still used as an ingredient in chocolate bars and chocolate desserts because it brings out the flavor of chocolate.

Vanilla Disease

People who work with large amounts of vanilla all day can catch a strange illness: vanillism. Vanilla's aroma is so strong that long exposure to it can cause headaches and allergic skin reactions.

Natural and Imitation Vanilla

True vanilla and its substitutes are quite different from one another. Vanilla-flavored products contain real vanilla extract. This flavoring is used so much in the food industry that chemists have developed artificial flavorings, which are much less expensive than the natural product. These substances do not have the subtle flavor of true vanilla.

THE PRESERVATION OF MILK

Almost all milk is pasteurized before it is sold. The process is named after the nineteenth-century French chemist Louis Pasteur, who discovered a method to destroy the bacteria that make food spoil. His discoveries were applied to canning and wine making as well as to milk. To pasteurize milk, it is heated to a temperature below boiling and then cooled. This kills the germs that could make people sick. It also kills the harmless organisms that make milk go sour quickly, so pasteurized milk can be kept longer than raw milk. More recently, some milk has been ultrapasteurized—more heat is used—so that it remains fresh for up to six months.

Pasteurization is sometimes confused with homogenization. Homogenization breaks the fat particles in the milk into smaller particles. The process mixes the cream throughout the milk and prevents it from separating and floating to the top.

Milk does not just come from cows. Goats, sheep, camels, water buffalo, reindeer, and yaks also give milk. In fact, all female mammals produce milk, including whales.

Milk and milk products (yogurt, cheese) are rich in calcium, which is essential to the proper growth of teeth and bones. To absorb about 500 mg of calcium, it is necessary to consume 1 glass of milk, 3/4 cup of yogurt, or 1 to 2 ounces of cheese. Milk and its by-products are also rich in vitamins A, B_2, B_6, B_{12}, D, and E. Many adults, however, cannot digest milk because they no longer have the enzyme necessary to digest lactase, the sugar in milk.

INDEX OF RECIPES

10 9 8 7 6 5 4 3 2 1

Photo credits • © Adagp, Paris 1992, page 15 • © Adagp, Paris 1992 / Photothèque Magritte-Giraudon, page 39 • © P. Asset, Hatchette Pratique, pages 11, 23, 31, 38, 39, 55 • © Bridgeman / Giraudon, page 39 • © G. Dagli Orti, pages 22, 30, 31, 47 • © A. Descat / MAP, pages 38, 39, 54 • © FGP International Dairy Industry / Explorer, page 36 • © H. Fouque / Explorer, page 46 • © G. Laethem, page 14 • © Lauros-Giraudon, pages 14, 22, 46, 47 • © Modes et Travaux, page 23 • © Y. Monel / MAP, page 54 • © Sahuquet / MAP, page 54

Library of Congress Cataloging-in-Publication Data

Rosin, Arielle.
    Pizzas & punk potatoes / by Arielle Rosin; photographs by Daniel Czap; research by Etienne Collomb. —— 1st American ed.
      p.   cm. —— (Young gourmet)
    Includes index.
    Summary: Basic introduction to cooking, with additional historical and cultural background information.
    ISBN 0-395-68381-5
    1. Cookery——Juvenile literature. 2. Cookery——History——Juvenile literature. [1. Cookery.] I. Czap, Daniel, ill. II. Title. III. Series.
TX652.5.R6713 1994
641.5'123—dc20   93-24970   CIP   AC

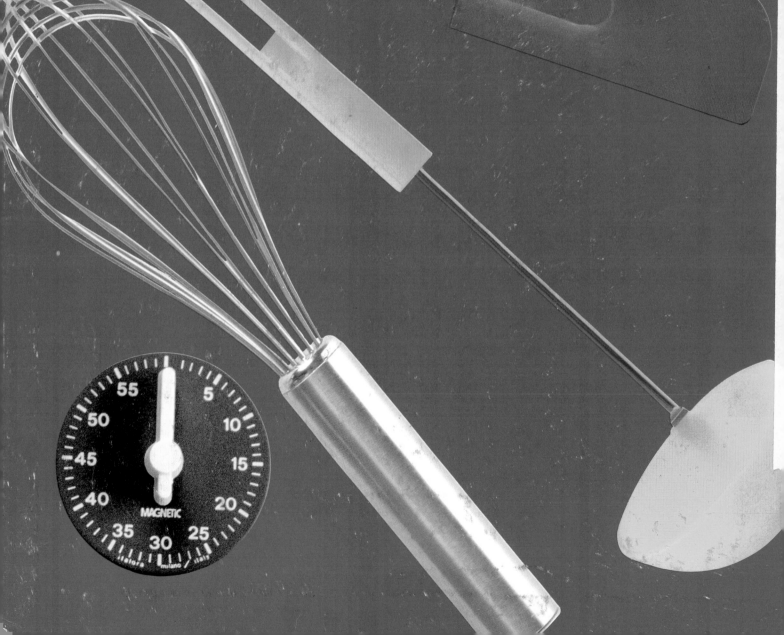